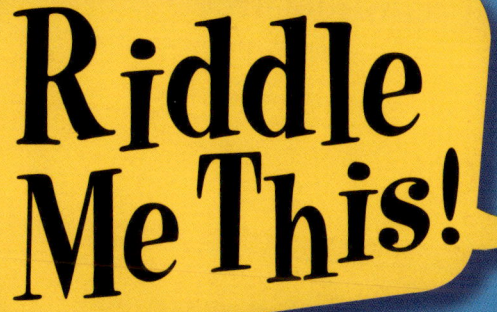

# Riddles at Home

Lisa Regan

WINDMILL BOOKS
NEW YORK

Published in 2015 by Windmill Books, An Imprint of Rosen Publishing, 29 East 21st Street, New York, NY 10010

Copyright © Arcturus Holdings Ltd.

All rights reserved. No part of this book may be reproduced in any form without permission in writing from the publisher, except by a reviewer.

First Edition

Text: Lisa Regan

Illustrations: Moreno Chiacchiera
 (Beehive Illustration)

Design: Notion Design

Editor: Joe Harris

Assistant editor: Frances Evans

US editor: Joshua Shadowens

Library of Congress Cataloging-in-Publication Data

Regan, Lisa, 1971-

 Riddles at home / by Lisa Regan. — First edition.

   pages cm — (Riddle me this!)

 Includes index.

 ISBN 978-1-4777-9169-1 (library binding) — ISBN 978-1-4777-9170-7 (pbk.) — ISBN 978-1-4777-9171-4 (6-pack)

 1. Riddles, Juvenile. 2. Dwellings—Juvenile humor. 3. Housekeeping—Juvenile humor. I. Title.

 PN6371.5.R4653 2015

 818'.602—dc23

Printed in the United States

SL004085US

CPSIA Compliance Information: Batch # AS4102WM: For Further Information contact Windmill Books, New York, New York at 1-866-478-0556

# Contents

Riddles .................................. 4

Answers ................................ 28

Glossary, Further Reading,
Websites, and Index ............. 32

Riddles at Home

**1** If a red house is made of red bricks and a brown house is made of brown bricks, what is a green house made of?

**2** What goes up and down the stairs without moving?

**3** I turn around once,
What is out will not get in.
I turn around again,
What is in will not get out.
What am I?

Answers on page 28

**4** What comes with a car, goes with a car, is of no use to the car, but the car cannot go without it?

**5** There are two in a corner, but only one in a room; there is one in an apartment and one in a shelter, but none in a mansion. What is it?

**6** What kind of transportation has eight wheels but can only carry one passenger?

**7** What has six wheels and flies?

Riddles at Home

Answers on page 28

## Riddles at Home

**8** I ask no questions, but you feel the need to answer me. What am I?

**9** I sing when I'm struck or whenever they shake me. By mold and cast, the craftsmen make me.

**10** What do you break just by saying its name?

**11** What do you call a man who stands outside the front door all day?

Answers on page 28

## 12 Mystery Word

EACH LINE OF THIS PUZZLE IS A CLUE TO A LETTER. CAN YOU DISCOVER THE HIDDEN WORD?

My first is in bread but never in dear,
My second's in yell and also in cheer.
My third is in duffle and also in hood,
My fourth is in word but isn't in wood.
My fifth and my sixth are letters the same.
A baboon and a rooster have two in their name.
My last is in temper and moody and slam.
My whole is at home—do you know where I am?

Riddles at Home

**13** What advice do you get from your hands?

Answers on page 28

Riddles at Home

**14** What belongs to you, but other people use it much more than you do?

**15** You have to poke me in the eye to get me to do what you want. I often live in a box, but you'd never find me in a haystack. What am I?

**16** Toby's mom went into the hospital to have her appendix removed. His sister went into the hospital a month later to have her tonsils taken out. A week after that, Toby needed a growth from his head removed. Why didn't he go to the hospital, too?

Answers on page 28

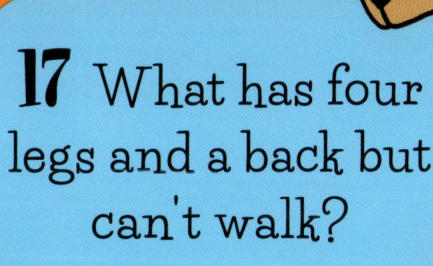

**17** What has four legs and a back but can't walk?

**18** I am buried in wood from one end to the other, but my head is on show while I hold things together. Do you know what I am?

**19** Divided, we are four families —two are red and two are black. What are we when we are together?

**20** I am very good at what I do, I do my job whenever you want, And I'm always on time ... But nobody likes me. What am I?

Riddles at Home

Answers on page 28

Riddles at Home

**21** What is two feet long but can be all different sizes?

**22** What is being described here?
When I am full, I can point the way,
But when I am empty, I lie still.
I keep you warm on a snowy day,
But I'm useless when it's sunny.

**23** Why did the computer nerd throw away his shirt?

**24** What has a neck but no head, and two arms but no hands?

Answers on page 28

**25** Why are warm and comfortable indoor shoes just like banana skins?

*Riddles at Home*

**26** I have a tongue but no mouth. I am no good to you on my own. What am I?

**27** When is a coat no use to keep out the cold?

**28** What is shown here?
Wear
Clean

11

Answers on page 29

## Riddles at Home

**29** What five-letter word becomes shorter when you add two letters to it?

**30** A pill and a cry of pain—put them together, and you can rest your sore head. What am I?

**31** What has a head and a tail, but no legs?

**32** Rosie's mom has three daughters. She has chosen their names carefully. The oldest is named April, and the middle one is named May. What is the youngest one called?

Answers on page 29

## 33 Mystery Word

EACH LINE OF THIS PUZZLE IS A CLUE TO A LETTER. CAN YOU DISCOVER THE HIDDEN WORD?

My first is in large and also in big,
My second's in wait but isn't in twig.
My third is in car, and in ride, and in truck,
My fourth is in sat but isn't in stuck.
My fifth is in gas but isn't in tanks,
My sixth is in creaks but isn't in cranks.
Figure out the letters and write each one down;
My whole can be found by a house or in town.

**Riddles at Home**

**34** Which burns longer, a short, fat candle or a tall, thin one?

Answers on page 29

## Riddles at Home

**35** Sally throws a ball as hard as she can, but it comes straight back to her without bouncing off of anything. How did she do it?

**36** What is served but never eaten?

**37** There are eight of us
To move at will,
We protect our king
From any ill.
What are we?

14

Answers on page 29

**38** What do a zipper, a comb, and a shark all have in common?

**39** What is as round as a frying pan and as deep as a sink, yet all the oceans in the world couldn't fill it up?

**40** There is one that has a head without an eye, And there's one that has an eye without a head. You may find the answer if you try: Half of what you seek hangs upon the thread.

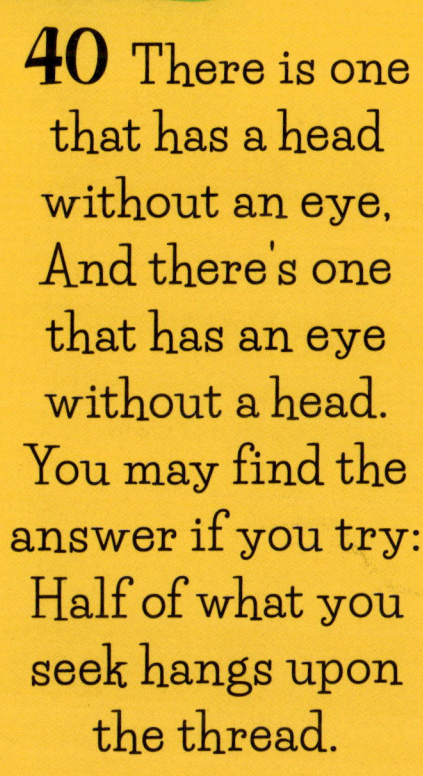

Riddles at Home

Answers on page 29

Riddles at Home

**41** A mom has two sons who share a birthday and were born in the same year—but they are not twins. How could this happen?

**42** How can you tell that birthdays are good for you?

**43** What has a face and two hands but no arms or legs?

**44** What time of day is the same spelled backward and forward?

Answers on page 29

**45** Ava has bought presents for her two sisters. Both presents do the same thing. One has many moving parts, but the other has none. One works all the time, but the other doesn't work at night. What did she buy?

**46** What word begins and ends with an "e" but only has one letter in it?

**47** What stays in the corner but travels around the world?

**48** Which month has 28 days?

Riddles at Home

Answers on page 30

## Riddles at Home

**49** If you screw a light bulb into a socket by turning the bulb clockwise with your right hand, which way would you turn the socket with your left hand in order to unscrew it while holding the bulb still?

**50** What has rivers but no water, cities but no people, and forests but no trees?

**51** What do extraterrestrial cats drink their milk from?

**52** What is always hot, even if you keep it in the fridge?

Answers on page 30

**53** Please don't drop me, or I will crack.
Give me a smile, and I'll always smile back.
What am I?

**54** What gets wetter the more it dries?

**55** What is full of holes but holds water?

**56** What can you find in the bathroom, in music, and on a snake?

Riddles at Home

Answers on page 30

## Riddles at Home

**57** Tom and Harry are sitting on opposite sides of the kitchen table. The table is the only thing between them, their eyes are open, and the lights are on—so why can't they see each other?

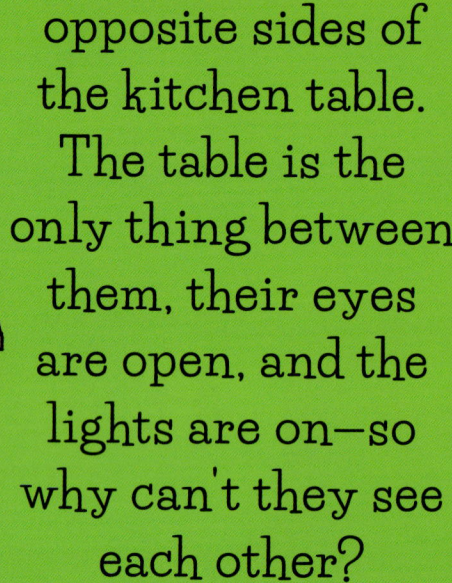

**58** You have a bag with four apples in it. You want to give an apple each to your mom, dad, brother, and sister. How can you do that and still have an apple left in the bag?

**59** When can you add 2 to 11 to get 1? (No fractions or negative numbers needed!)

Answers on page 30

**60** Jill and her friend Jack always tease each other. This time, Jill says to Jack, "If you sit on that chair, I bet I can make you stand up before I have run around the chair three times." Jack knows what Jill is like and makes her promise not to tickle him or even touch him. "I promise," says Jill. "When you get out of the chair, it will be totally your own choice." Jack accepts the challenge, but Jill wins the bet. How does she do it?

Riddles at Home

**61** Fill me with air, and I fly,
But fill me too much, and I die.
What am I?

Answers on page 31

## Riddles at Home

**62** Chris goes to the store to buy something for his house. One would cost him $1.50 and two would cost the same, but 12 would cost him $3 and 122 would cost him $4.50. What is he buying?

**63** I can be "cracked," I can be "played," I can be "taken," I can be "made." What am I?

**64** Poke your fingers in my eyes, and I will open my jaws for you. Cloth, leather, cardboard, or paper, I greedily devour them all.

Answers on page 31

**65** I have space but no room, and keys but no locks. I can return without leaving. I can shift without moving. I never speak, but there's no word I can't make. What am I?

Riddles at Home

**66** What room in the house will never have ghosts?

**67** What brings things to life, is never alive, but can still die?

**68** What has a spine but no bones, and leaves but no seeds?

Answers on page 31

## 69 Mystery Word

EACH LINE OF THIS PUZZLE IS A CLUE TO A LETTER. CAN YOU DISCOVER THE HIDDEN WORD?

My first is in kitchen and counter and hot,
My second's in zero and also not.
My next is in baking and bread and in taste,
My fourth is in rubbish and also in waste.
For my fifth, you write down my first once again,
For my sixth, find a letter in duke and in reign.
My last is in cherry but never in cheesy,
My whole helps you cook something yummy but easy.

**70** When is a door not a door?

**71** Three brothers share a family sport:
A nonstop marathon.
The oldest one is fat and short
And trudges slowly on.
The middle brother's tall and slim
And keeps a steady pace.
The youngest runs just like the wind,
Speeding through the race.
"He's young in years, we let him run,"
The other brothers say,
"Cause though he's surely number one,
He's second, in a way." Why is that?

**72** Can you name ten body parts spelled with three letters?

Riddles at Home

Answers on page 31

Riddles at Home

**73** Madison and Melissa were making snowballs ready to have a snowball fight. "Ready?" asked Melissa. "No way!" said Madison. "You have three times more snowballs than me!" So Melissa handed over a snowball. "You still have twice as many as me!" said Madison. How many more snowballs must Melissa give to Madison so they have the same number?

**74** I can go up a chimney when I'm down, but I could never go down a chimney when I'm up. What am I?

Answers on page 31

### Try these tongue twisters:

Which wristwatches are Swiss wristwatches?

Good blood, bad blood.

Flash message! Flash message!

Whether the weather be cold, or whether the weather be hot,
Whether the weather be warm, or whether the weather be not...
We'll weather the weather, whatever the weather,
Whether we like it or not!

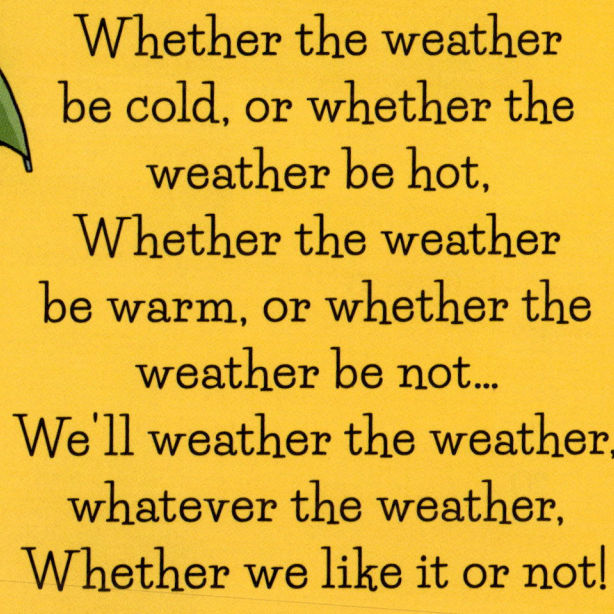

Riddles at Home

# Answers

## Page 4
1. Glass!
2. The carpet.
3. A key.

## Page 5
4. The noise of the car's engine.
5. The letter "r."
6. Roller skates.
7. A garbage truck (it is surrounded by flies—the insects—because of the trash).

## Page 6
8. The doorbell or the telephone.
9. A bell.
10. Silence.
11. Matt!

## Page 7
12. Bedroom.
13. Fingertips!

## Page 8
14. Your name.
15. A needle.
16. He just went to the hairdresser for a haircut.

## Page 9
17. A chair.
18. A nail.
19. A deck of cards.
20. An alarm clock.

## Page 10
21. A pair of shoes.
22. A glove.
23. Because nothing happened when he pressed the buttons.
24. A turtleneck sweater.

# Answers

### Page 11
**25** Because they are slippers!
**26** A shoe.
**27** When it's a coat of paint.
**28** Clean underwear.

### Page 12
**29** "Short."
**30** A pillow: "pill" + "ow."
**31** A coin.
**32** Rosie.

### Page 13
**33** Garage.
**34** Neither—candles burn shorter.

### Page 14
**35** She threw the ball straight up in the air.
**36** A tennis ball.
**37** Pawns in a chess game.

### Page 15
**38** Teeth.
**39** A colander or sieve.
**40** A pin and a needle.

### Page 16
**41** They are two sons out of triplets (or more).
**42** The more you have, the longer you'll live!
**43** A clock.
**44** Noon.

# Answers

## Page 17

**45** A clock and a sundial. They both tell the time, but the sundial does not work at night.
**46** Envelope.
**47** A stamp.
**48** All of them! And some have even more ...

## Page 18

**49** Clockwise. It doesn't matter which hand you use, but it does matter whether you're turning the bulb or the socket.
**50** A map.
**51** Flying saucers.
**52** Chili sauce.

## Page 19

**53** A mirror.
**54** A towel.
**55** A sponge.
**56** Scales.

## Page 20

**57** They have their backs to each other.
**58** Give an apple to your mom and one to your dad, hand one to your brother ... and give the bag with the last apple in it to your sister.
**59** On a clock: 11:00 plus 2 hours is 1:00.

# Answers

### Page 21
**60** When Jack sits down, Jill runs around the chair twice and then says, "I'll come back tomorrow to run around it a third time!"
**61** A balloon or a bubble.

### Page 22
**62** He is buying house numbers to put on the door.
**63** A joke.
**64** Scissors.

### Page 23
**65** A computer keyboard.
**66** The living room!
**67** A battery.
**68** A book.

### Page 24
**69** Toaster.
**70** When it's ajar!

### Page 25
**71** They're the hands on a clock.
**72** Arm, leg, eye, ear, lip, hip, gum, jaw, rib, toe.

### Page 26
**73** Two more. Madison started with three snowballs, and Melissa started with nine.
**74** An umbrella.

## Glossary

**appendix** (uh-PEN-diks) A small pouch-like body part that is joined to the gut.

**colander** (KOH-len-der) A bowl with small holes in it that is used for washing or draining food.

**craftsmen** (KRAFTS-men) Experts in a particular craft or trade.

**duke** (DOOK) A high-ranking nobleman.

**extraterrestrial** (EKS-trah-tuh-RES-tree-ahl) Something that does not come from Earth.

**mansion** (MAN-shun) A very large, impressive house.

**marathon** (MAR-uh-thon) A long-distance race.

**mold** (MOHLD) A hollow container used to give shape to a liquid as it hardens.

**tonsils** (TONT-sulz) Two small masses found on either side of the throat.

## Further Reading

Burbank, Lizzy. *Jokes for Kids: 299 Funny and Hilarious Clean Jokes for Kids.* North Charleston, SC: CreateSpace Independent Publishing, 2013.

National Geographic Kids. *Just Joking: 300 Hilarious Jokes, Tricky Tongue Twisters, and Ridiculous Riddles.* Des Moines, Iowa: National Geographic Society, 2012.

## Websites

For web resources related to the subject of this book, go to: www.windmillbooks.com/weblinks and select this book's title.

## Index

**B**
bathroom 19
birthdays 16

**C**
candle 13
car 5, 13
cloth 22

**D**
door 6, 24, 31

**F**
family 25

**H**
hospital 8
house 4, 13

**M**
mystery words 7, 13, 24

**P**
present 17

**S**
sport 25

**T**
table 20